Nikki and the Magic Well

"And a child shall lead them."
Nikki has discovered the secrets to obtaining generational wealth. Determined to share the tools to financial freedom with her mother, Nikki fights the many urges that life throws her way. Her journey home shines light on the many issues we face today.

AF720563

For permission requests, send an email to: email: Info@iammsclassy.com

First Printing

ISBN Hardcover: ISBN: 979-8-218-07418-0

www.lammsclassy.com

(ring) [the school bell rings] Yay! It's officially the weekend, says Nikki. She grabs her backpack and runs towards the door. I'm going to have so much fun this weekend. I have a list of things to do. She pulls out her to-do list as she begins to walk home.

Hey, what is that? Nikki sees a green glowing light above her head. She runs and follows the glowing light. Not paying attention to where she was running Nikki trips and falls into a well. Wooooah! Nikki screams out until there is a loud splash from the well.

Awe man! My mom is going to kill me, says Nikki as she squeezes water out of her hair. Wow! where am I? asked Nikki as her eyes grew bigger with amazement. She was sitting inside of a glowing well. The water was filled with lily pads that looked like money and above her head were floating coins. This is so cool, said Nikki.

The coins above Nikki's head began to spin around in circles. The glowing water started to make a big swirl. What's happening? Asked Nikki. Oh no, this can't be good, says Nikki. The coins began to spin faster and the glowing water started to swirl harder.

Little Nikki tried to hold on but there was nothing inside the well to grab onto. The glowing water swirled so hard that it shot Nikki straight up into the air. "Aaaah!" screams Nikki. The spinning coins then pushed Nikki straight down to the ground. (Thud!)

Uugh! What happened moaned Nikki holding her head.
Huh? Where did all of these numbers come from?
Nikki was surrounded by numbers and symbols.
This is so awesome! It's like a play book to getting a
big house. I have to tell my mom about this.
Nikki takes off running.

On her journey home Nikki passes a store that has a designer bag in the window. Look! It's on sale. She goes into the store and asks for the price of the designer bag. "It's on sale for 40% off," says the salesman. He scans the tag on the designer bag, beep! Your total is $3000. Will you be paying cash? Asked the salesman. Nikki's hands began to itch. 0h no! I better hurry home, says Nikki as she runs out of the store.

Nikki is waiting at a crosswalk for it to be safe to cross the street. A shiny sports car pulls up at the light and Nikki is in shock. What a beauty! Says Nikki. I can see myself on the side of the car. It's so shiny. The car takes off and turns into a car dealership. Nikki follows the car. "I have to touch it."

She walks into the car dealership and asks the sales lady "how much is the shiny car?" "Oh don't worry about it, we approve everyone" says the sales lady. "Really? Cool" says Nikki. "Yes, we just need $5000 down and you'll be able to make monthly payments of $800 a month." Nikki's hands began to itch again. "Oh, I need to get home fast." Nikki runs out of the car dealership and heads home.

Almost to her house Nikki sees a huge building with a flag on it. There was a creepy man standing outside the building wearing a tall hat. “Hey there, what's your name?” asked the man. “I’m Nikki, what’s your name?” replied Nikki. “My name is Boudreaux and I’m here to make all of your dreams come true,” replied the creepy man. “All of them?” Asked Nikki. “Oh yes,” answered the creepy man. “ All you have to do is step right inside of this building and I will make all of your dreams come true.”

Nikki began to dance with excitement. Now I can get a designer bag, a shiny car, and a big house for my mom and I. “As you wish," said Boudreaux. Come step inside for a 36 year long relationship that will change you and your mom‘s life, said Boudreau as he opened the door. Nikki looked inside and saw a sign that said “bank.” All of a sudden Nikki's hand begins to itch. “Uh oh! Not again” says Nikki and she turns around and runs down the street.

“Finally! Home sweet home,” sighs Nikki. She races up the apartment stairs to tell her mom about the numbers she sees and all of the tempting obstacles that come along with the magical numbers. “Mom, I'm home!” Shouts Nikki as she opens the door to apartment number 8312.

Finally, home sweet home. [illegible] Nikki. We raced up the apartment stairs to tell Mom and Dad about the numbers we saw and all of the addition and subtraction that came along with the magical numbers. "Mom, I'm home!" [illegible] Nikki as she opened the door to apartment number [illegible]?

Tina Nikki's mom was in the kitchen preparing dinner. "Hey sweetheart! How was your day? And why are you soaking wet?" Tina questions. "Mom there was a magic well of numbers and I accidentally fell in and now I can see magic numbers everywhere." "Wow! Slow down Nikki," says Tina. "Numbers aren't magic babygirl. They are just numbers. Now go and wash up for dinner" says Tina. "But Mom! Numbers are just numbers if you don't know the secret codes to unlock the magic. And I have the codes floating around me right now." Tina looks at Nikki with a confused face.

"Look at this mom" says Nikki as she grabs a crayon and a piece of paper. "You always say that you want a designer bag but they are too expensive. If you use the secret code to unlock the magic you can get the bag without spending your own money. Plus you'll get good girl points that you can use to buy us groceries since you say food is expensive." Tina stops and looks at Nikki, "where did you hear this from?" Asked Tina.

"It's all from the Magic well" replied Nikki.

"You can get a shiny car so that you don't have to keep taking our car to the shop. All you have to do is pay all the bills on time to get a high score. Then they'll give you a shiny new car for your prize."

Tina sits down at the dinner table and stares at Nikki.

"But that's not the best part!" Says Nikki beaming with excitement. "Because you pay the bills on time, and got the designer bag and the shiny car you'll get a super high score and this time your prize can be a big house."
Tina smiles at Nikki and says, "you're so awesome."
Nikki hugs her mom and says "no mom, credit is awesome."

www.ingramcontent.com/pod-product-compliance
Lightning Source LLC
LaVergne TN
LVHW080002210926
848481LV00012B/3650
979821807418O